MOTIVATION DRIVES SUCCESS

SUCCESS

VOL 1

MOTIVATE YOURSELF TOWARDS SUCCESS,
ORGANIZATION & PRIORITIZATION

WHY YOU SHOULD READ THIS BOOK

A lot of people go after goals in business or in life only to find themselves not making progress and losing their drive. Think of all the broken New Years Resolutions people make each year. Why is that? Your goal may be fine, but you may not have a good enough reason to go for it. That is, you may lack real motivation.

This book will practically show you step by step process to drive yourself towards success through organizing and prioritizing, there by providing you the right guardian to overcome every motivational related issues. Consequently improviing your overall well being…

TABLE OF CONTENTS

Introduction

Motivation is key to success and there are no two thoughts about it. When we start out to do something, there is a motivation but as we move, our thoughts propel several excuses to counter it. In order to reach a motivation level you desire, you need to be a practical thinker and not just a plain dreamer.

Whether your goals are for your career, social life, health or personality development, self motivation holds the key. You must always be eager to find out what motivates you and must build upon that to reach your goals. Motivation is achieved or maintained by different people in different ways. Some get motivated by inspirational books, while some others get motivated by biographies or observing great people.

Life in its entirety can never be fully planned nor can we always realize all our desires. There are times in our life when we are down. Life is not only about winning; it is also about how we cope with our losses. To achieve our aims, we need to build a continuous motivation drive.

First things first, BELIEVE, LOVE, & TRUST YOURSELF, knowing that you have the power to achieve everything that your heart desires. When you believe that you can accomplish the task at hand, you naturally become driven to succeed.

In order to succeed it is vital that you motivate yourself; it is not wise to always depend on others to motivate you. Here are reasons why it is important that you motivate yourself for your success:

- It Gives You Control: When you motivate yourself, you don't have to wait for someone else to do it for you. You can determine when you will do what it takes to move forward and then take corresponding action immediately.

- It Helps You Get Through The Difficulties In Life: With self motivation you are able to inspire yourself to take action in the midst of problems and difficult situations. This means you don't have to wait for things to change before you are able to make your next move. Because you are motivated from within, you are compelled to keep going and your inner drive is not predicated on outside situations and circumstances. You can then navigate through the challenges without stopping thus increasing your chances of succeeding faster.

- It Provides You With A Sense Of Purpose And Direction: Your motivation is fueled by whatever inspires you. When you have motivation fueled by inspiration you have purpose. As a result, you know what you are striving to be, do or have. And that dream will push you in the direction of its attainment.

- It Provides Enthusiasm And Excitement In Life: When you motivate yourself, you will feel happier about doing the work than you would if you had to rely on someone else to motivate you. You need to cultivate the habit of doing things for your own reasons. If for example, you had to mow your lawn, you would enjoy it more if you did it for your own reasons than you would if you waited until someone else tried to talk you into doing it.

- It Gives You The Ability To Live A Fulfilling Life: Self motivation usually comes from an emotional desire. You need to let that desire motivate you. It will cause you to do whatever needs to be done to accomplish your objectives. Once you eventually succeed, you will feel fulfilled because the inner motivation stemmed from a burning desire that you had an emotional attachment to.

Motive: what is your motive for doing what you're doing; where does your motivation come from; can you get to that place inside you where the real strength comes from? After all the hype is gone, what is left is what's inside– the inspirations that guide you to do whatever it is you want to do. You need to have that quiet place where you can turn off the outside environment to find yourself. Write about yourself, your goals, your inspirations, and get some realizations about yourself. This will give you a better insight as to what it is that you want out of life.

Just like anybody who has ever been inspired throughout history to accomplish something great, the passion does not come from the mind. Rather, motivation is a fire that burns inside of you, and it is essential that you find this power. This is what will drive you and keep you on the path to success. So take notes constantly; could be be anything ranging from ideas, thoughts, plans to future projects and ways you can improve various aspects of your life that you want to change.

People are motivated by different things. Some are motivated by money while some others are motivated by fear. It is therefore important to understand that what motivates one may not motivate another. In our journey to achieving success, there will be obstacles in the path of our motivation and one single effective way of eliminating obstacles is taking action. People need to take action to pursue their goals, and not put things off. The amazing thing is you can achieve success in an instant or at a particular moment but you would never know it if you fail to take action.

Pertinent questions to ask are : how do you move towards your motivations, what are you going to do to change where you are right now to where you want to be in the future? These questions and more are answered in the book but endeavor to remember this: *Winners take imperfect actions, while losers worry about perfecting the action.*

For starters, let's focus on getting organized so that we can create a clear path to accomplishing our goals. When you think about your goals, try and visualize any obstacles in your way; ignore the mental obstacles by focusing on physical barriers. A large part of our frustration and lack of forward momentum come from our own negative thoughts. You see, we tend to overthink things instead of staying focused on the goal. If we allow ourselves to place mental blocks on our path to accomplishment, we subconsciously focus all our attention on these blocks rather than the initial goal we set for ourselves thus cluttering our path to success. The remaining part of the book will be examining ways by which you can organize and prioritize in order to motivate yourself toward success with one chapter dedicated to each new way. Keep reading and find out more.

Chapter 1:

Goal Setting

Be realistic and kind to yourself. If you wish to see yourself succeed, do not create a situation only a super-hero may accomplish. Set your final goal and work towards it by creating a step-by-step timeline. Achieving a goal is like learning a new skill, which is time-dependent; goals like educational milestones, weight loss,and traveling can be attained within a defined timeframe. Other kinds of goals like spiritual growth and developing healthy habits might continue throughout your life.

We would probably ask what drives a person to get something that he wants. One of the possible answers is goal setting and there are many aspects to consider when setting goals in life.

Each of us have distinctive goals that fit our personality when trying to achieve a certain kind of objective. There are two types of goals, the long-term and short-term goals. The outcomes of short-term goals are usually temporary in nature; a good example is a set of routine tasks that we need to complete in a day.

Conversely, long-term goals have effects that last for a long time or can be used for future undertakings. A good example is buying your own house in two years time or finishing college in in the next three years. Goals differ and they mean different things to different people. Sometimes, the goals we choose are based on our current position and subsequently affect our wants in life.

Our dream in life also plays a vital role when it comes to setting our goals. We should set certain margins and boundaries for the extent to which we will like to go in order to achieve our goals. This is because taking too much of anything we want can result to greediness. In doing so, we might just be activating self-destructon for ourselves.

In general, people who have a stronger motivational drive tend to work harder and strive to do better. Keeping yourself on the right direction and a persistent mindset makes you reach whatever your desires are. Scarcity in life is something that can urge a person to do his best. Such a person has virtually nothing and thus, sets up a firm goal from the existing need of improving the way he or she lives. It is therefore possible that such people tend to have more long term-goals than short-term goals as that suits them more.

Those who are born with a silver spoon have another kind of view when it comes to goal setting. They are more likely to come up with short-range objectives since they already have material stuffs in abundance and also because they will always expect to have what they want immediately.

In order to get your goals with less hassle, you should have an optimistic state of mind. The major thing is to attain it without hurting anyone else along the road. Being true to all your intentions makes you successful in your undertakings and you'll be able to get what you want.

With any type of goal, it helps to write down specifically what progressive steps you would like to achieve within a particular time frame. Don't take on more than you may handle too soon, particularly if your goal is something outside your knowledge or present ability. It's easy to get disheartened when you recognize that your goal of running three miles a day has petered out after two weeks because you can't seem to get past one mile a day. Unless you've been an active runner, it's better to start slow and work your way up in increments.

There is something you need to take note of when it comes to setting goals and writing them down; that is the kind of words you use because words are quite powerful. It is therefore imperative that you analyze and choose your words carefully; using words like *try, may, should, might* gives the impression of reluctance and holding back, attitudes that are not befitting of winners. Winners don't overthink things, they simply take action; so, if you want to achieve your goals and be a winner, then you need to do away with words that will not instigate definite action such as the ones earlier mentioned. To overcome your obstacles, break them down into small parts; this is one of the secrets to creating that desired reality for yourself.

For example, if you want to raise your income from $10,000 to $30,000 and you're finding obstacles in your way. Do not panic; just break the process down into steps by probably starting with increasing your income to $11,000 or $12,000 rather than focusing on getting $30,000. Once you're able to attain the first form of increment, you only need to be consistent with what you're doing until you reach your goal.

When we are looking to manifest our goals, simply take a quality you want in your life and focus on achieving it. Say for example, you're trying to turn one dollars to thousands or millions of dollars, it's best to take it one at a time so that you don't become overwhelmed. Sometimes, in your journey to success, you have to stop, change positions and see all the different areas from other perspectives. Put yourself in the mindset as if you have a million dollars and look at it from that perspective even though you are broke.

If you get your mind to believe, the monetary value is insignificant. It doesn't matter if it's $1 or $100,000, believing with your subconscious will manifest it into your reality. It is the same road to travel whether you are where you want to be or are stuck. It is in your thoughts that you can create the motivation to get bold! You can do whatever it is you put your mind to! Do it big! Be unreasonable and just go for it. When you begin small and set mini-goals for yourself, you're much more likely to succeed.

CHAPTER 2:

UTILIZE TO-DO LISTS

Take charge of your time. When utilized properly, a to-do list gives you a specific idea of what you have to accomplish. How many times have you gotten someplace only to forget what you needed in the first place? Writing a to-do list saves time, energy, and even tension. A great list lets you forget the unimportant factors and once you have a written reminder, your brain is free to center on your goals.

To-do lists can be your best friend or your worst enemy. There's a modicum of pure satisfaction that comes from crossing through to-dos, that feeling you get at the end of the day when you've checked everything off the list. In addition to that, your productivity skyrockets when you use them effectively. But a poorly managed and unrealistic task list, on the other hand, can leave you feeling overwhelmed and ready to give up.

managing your to-do lists

1. Find an accountability partner

Sometimes, an item on the to-do list might get pushed back because something more important came up. But too often, we like to justify a moment of procrastination by calling it "prioritization." There's a big difference between those two terms. To stay on track, I suggest finding an accountability partner who can hold you to achieving the goals you set for yourself.

2. Identify three top priorities each day.

Once you write your long to-do list, highlight the three things you must accomplish in order to be productive and priority-focused that day. Don't fall for the thrill of easy wins.

3. Estimate the time it takes to complete each task

If you have downtime between meetings, for example, you can easily knock off a few items on your to-do list if you estimate they will each take a couple of minutes to complete. When you have longer available blocks of time, you can focus on heavier tasks that might take between 30 minutes and several hours to complete.

4. Create a "to-don't list"

The problem with to-do lists? Things just get in the way! Here's the fix: Alongside your to-do list, create a "to-don't" list. These are things you need to not do in order to accomplish your tasks for the day, such as "Don't open email before 10 a.m.," "Don't eat a heavy lunch" and "Don't answer phone calls while focusing."

5. Schedule each action item on your calendar

A to-do list is only as effective as the action you put behind it, and the best way to get things done is to schedule them on your calendar. When you know something needs to be done, set aside time to do it. If it's something that can be done quickly, do it immediately. If it takes more time than you have at that moment, then schedule it on your calendar against when you have time.

6. Make it digital

In today's digital age, you don't have to limit your to-do list to pen and paper. Task management systems can allow you to create virtual to-do lists with deadlines, priorities, multiple tasks and much more. Most of these are simple, intuitive and don't require a computer expert to set up. Don't limit yourself to when it comes to something as important as your productivity.

7. Review your list at the start and end of each day

Schedule time at the end of each day to evaluate your to-do list. What was accomplished? Cross it off. What's still pending? What's the priority? Cull, organize and prioritize the list. At the beginning of each day, review the task list that you left prepared and schedule out your day based on your to-do list and priorities.

8. Focus on one thing at a time

Too often, we make a to-do list with every thought that comes into our minds, which leads to long and detailed lists that can be daunting. The key to an effective to-do list is to prioritize the list and then focus on a singular task at a time. Don't overwhelm yourself by looking at the length of the list. Focus on the first task, then move down the list one step at a time.

9. Trim your list daily

A to-do list is for short-term tasks: single action items you intend to complete within seven days. Items that don't fit this criterion should be removed. If anything on your to-do list requires more than one action, it's a project. Remove it from your list and use a project management tool. Once an item is on your list for seven days, do one of the "3 D's": drop it, delegate it or do it immediately.

10. Use it for everything you do

Use the same list for work and play. When you combine work and personal activities (and that includes leisure time), you create a habit of using the list. Whether you jot tasks down on paper or use any one of the online to-do-list apps, the more consistently you use a list, the more effective it becomes. Big presentation due? Grocery lists? Doctor appointment? Everything needs to get done, so put them all on the same list.

11. Be realistic

The best thing to do is make the tasks on your to-do list realistic. As much as you would like to finish all of your current projects, most people overload the list and make it impossible to check each item off by the end of the day. Adjust your expectations so that you can feel good about crossing off those to-dos, making you feel more accomplished and refreshed.

CHAPTER 3:

ARRANGE FIRM DEADLINES

Setting a deadline forces you to work toward it. Set a definite date and time. Stating 'When I get a chance' or 'Sometime in the near future' is insufficient. Set your timeline for success and be specific with the desired result.

T is for TIMED. You need to set deadlines and timeframes for each goal. Once again, you need to be realistic, but you also need to push yourself. If you have a set date in mind to complete sub-goal one, you can maintain a high level of motivation without being overwhelmed. Once that sub-goal is achieved, you're one step closer.

Once again, you may need to do some research. Maybe you're writing about current farming practices? You could use the first three months to interview people in the industry, get yourself out there and gain real-life perspective. Write out a timeline and cross off each objective. If you find that you're moving too slowly, either reassess your timeline or push yourself even harder.

When it comes to companies, this is a big one, and it takes more guts than a lot of companies are willing to muster. But the fact of the matter is that working against a hard deadline can often be the very reason why your team never seems to meet a deadline. Your team is pressured by that hard date. They are unable to take time to explore alternatives that may produce a better end result. They're constantly feeling like they're up against a wall without an escape route and as such, their motivation and determination gets crushed.

If it's possible, consider doing away with hard dates in exchange for "great products that are shipped when they're ready". That's a value statement that anyone in your company can get behind. Nobody's going to stand up during a meeting and say that they'd prefer to ship a shoddy product faster, and if they do, then chances are that you've hired the wrong person.

If you absolutely can't kill your deadlines, then this is a quote for you,

"Sometimes the world demands something is ready on a certain date. My approach would still be to break the "thing" down into pieces that can be gracefully degraded, so that as much as possible it's of top quality"

HOW TO CONQUER YOUR FEAR OF DEADLINES

Start By Asking When, Not What; "What do you want done?" is usually the first question that gets asked when planning a project. After some discussion, you usually find out when the project needs to be finished.

However, sometimes a better opening question is "When do we want this done?" Start out by setting your deadline. Then, work backward to figure out how much you can realistically accomplish between that day and your deadline.

People don't like deadlines because they make them feel constrained and tied down. If you can master your deadlines by outlining and planning realistically what you can do, in a set timeframe, meeting deadlines will no longer be a burden to you or your organization.

1. Aim To Deliver, Not For Perfection

- Shoot for completion of projects quickly instead of shooting for perfection.
- Write down your deadline. You'll publish on this date whether it's perfect or not.
- If you work with a team gather everyone's ideas on your project.
- Share those ideas in a way everyone can see, and ask them to take a look. After they look or even miss their due date of looking, that's it. No more updates.
- Draft a blueprint of the project from those rough ideas.

- Get final approval for your project blueprint from the big wigs in your company.

- Ask the folks with sign-off authority a simple question: "If I deliver what you approved, on budget and on time, will you ship it?"

- Don't move forward until you get your yes. "Once you get your yes, go away and build your project, thrash-free. Ship on time, because that's what a linchpin does."

- While some of that relates to office bureaucracy, you get the idea. Start with a deadline, then give yourself permission to ship on time without excuses.

2. Create A List Of What Needs To Get Done (And When)

Setting and maintaining timeline and project goals is arguably one of the most challenging parts of being a project manager. Whether you're a one-person operation or have a large team, keeping all these tasks on track and moving forward takes some attention to detail.

3. Set Smaller Deadlines Within Your Large Deadline

Use these tips to break down your bigger deadlines into smaller ones:

• Look at the big picture and draw a road map of exactly what you need to do.

• Separate tasks based on who needs to complete them.

• Create an outline labeling what needs to be done and by when.

• Ask yourself what needs to be done in order? What can be done whenever?

• Delegate tasks based on who needs to do what, and then fill the gaps with tasks that can be done whenever.

4. Build In Buffer Time

Write down all the tasks you need done and the time needed for completion. Then, give each of these due dates a day or two of buffer room before they are actually due so you don't set yourself up for failure. This allows time to make needed changes, or even finish your work ahead of schedule.

5. Remember You Only Have So Much Room On Your Plate

This is one of those pieces of advice where it's a "do as I say and not as I do".

Everyone has 24 hours in a day; there are limitations to what can be done and what can be done well. You know your strengths and weaknesses, look at what is on your plate for the week and go from there.

This will help you to know exactly how much free time you have in the day and week, while keeping you accountable for meeting your personal deadlines, and helping you improve your time management skills.

This way, when someone comes to you with a new project or idea, you can look at your schedule and realistically know if you can fit one more thing on your plate or not. This will save you the stress and hassle of overburdening yourself.

Here's how to do it yourself:

Value all your time: Know that you have 24 hours every day, just like everyone else (even Beyoncè). Time spent hopping onto Facebook, texting, or in a mindless zone out all adds up. The average Facebook user spends 17 minutes on Facebook a day. That's 4 and a half days a year. Imagine how much you could get done in that extra time.

Focus on your work: While zoning out can distract from work, it's a proven fact that daydreaming can actually put off the desire for future rewards because you envisioned success but did nothing to achieve it. Being actionable helps you achieve your goals. Big game talk and day dreaming don't.

End procrastination:

- Start easy.

- Break it down.

- Be nice to yourself.

- Get a good why.

- Be mindful.

6. Work During Your Most Productive Hours

Emails, phone calls, instant messages etc. represent distractions which sometimes might make typical work hours not to be your most productive time of the day. This is because when you are constantly being interrupted, it's hard to put your head down and really work.

Many time-saving tricks say "put your phone away" or "log out of your email". Well, I don't know about you, but when I turn off my e-mail and phone, I get anxious. I feel like I'm going to miss something or someone needs me to take care of something, and I'm not getting my jobs done.

This constant worry is just as much of a distraction (if not more) as checking my email every hour. So, instead of turning off my phone, I just schedule the things I really need to focus on at night. It's the time I feel more awake and focused, and I can crank out things I want to do or other projects faster, with typically fewer distractions.

My method might not work for you as you might be a morning person. If you're such a person, get up early, reward yourself with a cup of your favorite coffee, and put your head down to tackle your biggest project for the day. And vice versa if you're a night owl.

You know yourself. Use your most productive hours to your advantage, and you'll be amazed by how much more you conquer in your day.

7. Never Push Deadlines

It's understandable that sometimes things happen that derail productivity. However, sometimes you just need to work faster or set more attainable deadlines.

It's really as simple as that.

Hitting deadlines isn't easy. However, nothing worth doing is easy. These tips and tactics can make getting things done on time much easier though.

CHAPTER 4:

FINISH EVERY DAY ON A GREAT NOTE

Save your simplest tasks for the end of every day. You'll be able to finish them, and end every day on a positive, rewarding note! On the bright side, little annoyances won't ruin an otherwise great day. If for example, you're stuck in traffic, you can utilize the time to finish an audio book or practice your singing or some other simple task that you need to complete.

CHAPTER 5:

REST AND UNWIND

Get a great night's sleep (seven hours or more.) Enough rest at night will help you to be alert, on schedule and effective the next day. Keep yesterday's concerns behind you. Try to take a couple of deep breaths and let yourself self-absorb for a while. Don't ever miss your time to rejuvenate for the next day; don't allow the thoughts of the day to take that away from you.

CHAPTER 6:

KEEP YOUR EYES ON THE PRIZE

As you begin to organize and prioritize your objectives, the desired outcome becomes more achievable because you're able to keep your eye on the prize. Obviously, the prize is whatever goal or task you are looking to accomplish. But to keep an eye on it, you first need to define it. You need a concrete plan that gives you a step-by-step direction on what it will take to solve your problem or accomplish a goal.

It's important to focus on the rewards and not the process. Most people tend to think about the process of doing it and this is what kills their motivation. When you think about the process such as the need to make cold calls, needing to wake up early in the cold weather and go for jogging, and some other things you might need to do in order to achieve a particular set of goals, this might make you feel down straight away. Therefore, focusing on the process is not going to help but rather think about the rewards you are going to get and you will be motivated right away.

Pursuing your dreams will help you avoid distracting temptations and enable you to focus on the subjects that mean the most to you.

Find a passion that inspires you to achieve greatness. Follow it and run with it, pushing out any obstacles and distractions that impede you from reaching your goal. Keep your eye on the prize! It's easy to succumb to temptation when your energy is not completely focused; so ensure to stay focused.

Chapter 7:

Set Up An Interview With An Experienced Person

Creating a concrete plan isn't an easy task. We aren't always familiar with what needs to get done in order to get to our goals. If this is the case, try to find someone who has done what you are trying to do; . If you can find someone, set up an interview with him or her. Be sure to have a list of questions ready before the interview. Try to keep the questions focused on accomplishing your goal. Ask about the kinds of roadblocks the person had to overcome and whether it took longer than anticipated. Don't be afraid to ask tough questions, as your aim is not to publish the interview but to gather insight. If they happen to push back, then you can scale it back a bit.

CHAPTER 8:

GET A MENTOR

Another possibility is finding a mentor or a coach who will help you set up your goals for you. Make sure this person is qualified in the field or area that you are working in. Coaches who are generalists may not be able to help you with specific situations that come up for you. Rather, you want someone who has been through it before. Of course, this depends entirely on what you are trying to accomplish. If it is general in nature, you could choose the generalist. You may also be able to find information online, and it can't hurt to do an initial search (which you probably already have done.) It's prudent when doing this, to take much of what you find with a grain of salt and fact-check as much as you can.

I've seen it over and over again in professional and personal life, finding an outstanding mentor can save you years of hard work, of trying to figure out how things work, what to focus on and how you can achieve your goals as quickly as possible, hoping to enjoy success in younger years.

Many times, having a mentor makes all the difference between making it in life or not. I mentored few people in my career and helped them go after goals they never thought were achievable to them; and today, they are successful individuals. All it took from my side was a little bit of guidance, push, faith and to foresee the potential they had.

On the other hand, my own past accomplishments and successes were accelerated the most by outstanding mentors and mastermind groups. I learned more from a few people in my life than I did from all others combined.

I agree that you can learn a lot from anybody, but only a few people can teach you the little tricks of life that put you on the fast lane to success.

Finding an outstanding mentor is not a mere stroke of luck, it should be a part of your life strategy, and the relationships you build in your life. If you want to be more successful in life, it's time that you get yourself a real mentor. I'll teach you how in few points:

- Why having a personal mentor is so important

- What to expect from a personal mentor

- How to find a mentor that will accelerate your success

- Things that will help you find a mentor

Relationships in your life are the most important influencers on your quality of life and how much you will achieve in your lifetime. This is why you must build your relationships strategically at least to some extent, and that also includes finding yourself an outstanding mentor.

WHY HAVING A MENTOR IS SO IMPORTANT

Imagine having a book in which you can find the exact recipe for succeeding in any area of life. The recipe can be for anything, from how to build a successful career in your industry to starting a profitable business, getting a six-pack in a few months, finding the love of your life or anything else you really want.

Imagine having a step-by-step guide in your hand that tells you how to achieve your goals with the least amount of effort, including with all the dirty secrets. An outstanding mentor, someone who already achieved what you want, is the closest you can get to that kind of guide. The closest because there is no way success can be exactly replicated, but it can definitely be modeled to a certain extent.

Even though success can't be 100% replicated, having a mentor is in many ways much better than having a success guide in the shape of a book; because a quality mentor doesn't only show you the way and share the real secrets of success with you, they also believe in you, boost your confidence, challenge you and push you right to the top of your performance. These are the things that only a mentor can do, and not a single book, guide or motivational video can do that.

The best athletes and businessmen in the world have mentors, so why wouldn't you? Based on the goals you want to achieve, there are many different kinds of mentors who can help you:

• Profession mentors – Mentors who do the same or similar job as you.

• Industry mentors – Industry experts who can help you understand market insights.

• Business-skills mentors – Mentors who help you with general business skills like sales, marketing, finance, negotiation and other important skills.

• Life-skills mentors – Mentors who help you master different life skills and be more successful in different areas of life, such as wealth, health, happiness etc.

• Technology mentors – Mentors who help you with the use of new technologies.

• Specialists Mentors – People you hire who are experts in specific areas, and by doing a service for you, they also transfer knowledge and wisdom to you (psychologists, lawyers, personal trainers etc.). No matter the type of mentor (s) you have, there are only three things you should look for in your mentor that really matter

- Someone who believes in you
- Someone who shows you the way
- Someone who brings out the best in you and challenges you

–Someone Who Believes In You

You've probably heard the phrase that you need at least one person to believe in you to become successful. The best option is if that person is you. It definitely helps if you believe in yourself, but it's often far from enough.

It's hard to believe in yourself all the time. Sooner or later, we all get crippled by doubts, insecurities, shame and other negative feelings. Doubt kills more dreams than failure ever will.

When you doubt yourself, the thing that can make the difference between following your dreams and giving up is having a more experienced person, an authority, or an expert who unconditionally believes in you and motivates you.

Doubt kills more dreams than failure ever will and mentors are far the best doubt killers.

People who have a healthy and encouraging environment in terms of empowering relationships don't give up. People without that kind of supportive environment give up sooner or later. It's that simple because it's not easy to succeed.

Life can easily break you down. There is no character in the world so strong that life couldn't break them with stress, challenges and misfortune. Only a supporting environment is what can help you to rise up fast and fight again.

The best teams in the world have the best coaches. The best athletes in the world have the best coaches. The best business individual will tell you that they would never work for someone they don't respect and can't learn from. If you want to be successful in life, you need a mentor– someone who believes in you when you don't and no one else does. So, when you find a mentor, make sure that they believe in you 100%. You can see it in their eyes if they really do.

Even superheroes in movies have mentors. Nobody can succeed alone; we all need somebody to be successful.

–Someone Who Shows You The Way

When you're new to something, be it a new industry, a new organization, or you're a newbie starting to take care of any life area, be it health, investment, relationship management or anything else, there is so much you don't know. There's always a long learning curve and being a newbie sucks.

You have to deal with wrong assumptions, distorted expectations, failure, setbacks, hard work, fast learning, always being behind others and many other psychologically extremely demanding challenges. That's why people rarely try something new because they can't handle the newbie apathy that usually lasts for months and months as well as the learning curve.

Besides pushing, encouraging and believing in you, the main point of having a mentor is to shorten your newbie apathy and learning curve. One of the main purposes of having a mentor is for them to point you in the right direction, focus your efforts, show you the little tricks and dirty life secrets, and guide you on the path toward your dreams.

You've probably heard the quote that good decisions come from experience and experience comes from making bad decisions. A mentor can share with you all the bad decisions they made in the past, so you don't have to repeat the same mistakes, and when you're with a mentor in person, they will share many more things with you than they'd write down in any book or share in any interview.

–Someone Who Brings Out The Best In You

A real mentor believes in you, boosts your confidence, encourages you, shows you the way, guides you, tells you life secrets, but is also tough on you. This is how a real mentor brings out the best in you; successful mentoring is always tough love.

Constant praise or commendation only makes you nothing but cocky with time and it never brings out the best in you. When you do something wrong or bad, a mentor should be honest, strict and direct with you; and then show you how to do it better. "And show you how to do it better" is a very important part.

If you don't listen to their advice and don't have a strong counterargument why, they should probably end the mentoring relationship immediately. The idea of mentorship is not small talk, but progress.

A good mentor should challenge you, push you, open your eyes to how you can achieve even more. And a good mentor knows that sometimes, it's necessary to kill any doubts and weaknesses in a very tough way when you're mentoring someone.

Choosing the right time to use encouragement and tough love is an art form, and rare are the people who know which to use when. Find a mentor who knows how to use both in the right situation.

The fact is that if you want to achieve your peak potential in any area of life, someone has to show you the world as it is, with all its pluses and minuses, in all its beauty and rottenness.

Many times, it's hard to accept reality. But living in your own naive dream world is the number one thing preventing you from progressing in life and achieving your peak performance.

The job of a great mentor is also to evict any wussiness from you, any soft and naive beliefs and behaviors. Now, that doesn't mean that a great mentor doesn't encourage you to be a good person, to always do the right thing and have integrity. It only means that a good mentor shows you how to not be your own biggest enemy in life; because many people are.

How To Find A Mentor

It's easy to find a mentor. It's very hard to find a really great mentor! The more successful the person you target as a mentor is, the more you have to be mentally prepared for real mentorship and advancement. You probably know the quote that when a student is ready, the teacher will appear.

It's easy to find a mentor but very hard to find a really great mentor! Nevertheless, when you decide to get a mentor in your life, you have to be proactive, not hoping that it will just happen. There are a few good ways of finding a mentor:

• Your job

• Direct contact (email, conferences)

• Professional coaches

• Mentoring programs

–YOUR JOB

The place where you work is one of the best opportunities for finding a mentor. First of all, never work for a boss you don't respect and can't learn from. If you have the abundance mindset, you know that there are many jobs out there and you deserve more than just a job.

You deserve a workplace where you can create, develop yourself, learn from other people and also earn decent money (if you provide enough value, of course).

Learn while you earn. Earn while you get mentored.

Many companies have mentoring programs and assign a mentor to every newcomer, but employees rarely take full advantage of such programs. Don't be one of them!

Be proactive and make sure that you get the most out of the mentoring program if your company provides one.

Set regular meetings with your assigned mentor, learn from them and show them your professionalism, ambitions and seriousness. Not only will you have a mentor, your chances for promotion will also be greater. Just don't be shy and passive.

If there is no such mentoring program in your company, analyze people you respect the most in the company and ask them directly if they're prepared to mentor you.

There's a great chance that they'll be honored and happy to do it. At the end of the day, you're in the same boat and it ends up being a win-win situation.

–Direct Contact (Email, Conferences, Etc.)

The next thing you can do is to carry out some research, find someone you really want to have as a personal coach and write to them or contact them directly.

You can approach them, for example, at a conference they lecture at, write them an email or make the initial contact another way.

If you aren't aiming for the top 1% or really busy people like presidents and blue-chip company CEOs, there are great chances that people will respond positively to you.

Sure you'll get rejected, but if you prepare a list of 20 potential mentors and write to them one by one, you'll get to a yes sooner or later.

–PROFESSIONAL COACHES

Many people dedicate their careers to personal coaching. You can easily find them online, either by using search engines or by browsing different personal coach directories.

It's definitely one of the best ways to find a mentor, even though mentoring sessions will not be free.

There are many advantages of professional coaching. Professional coaches usually have more experience with actual mentoring and coaching, they prepare better and they simply have to deliver results, because you pay them for that. If they don't deliver results, they won't stay in business for long.

The downside, besides paying for coaching, is that they have probably not achieved success in the area you want to succeed in; in essence, they are generalists, not specialists.

So if you need someone to mentor you in how to succeed in your industry or in a very specific thing, it may turn out that there are not many professional coaches with such a background. Nevertheless, you can still combine more different coaches and mentors to get the best possible result.

Well, if you try a professional coach or two and see how things go, you don't have a lot to lose. You know the philosophy: try it and see for yourself how it works. And you don't need to have a professional coach constantly.

In my experience, people usually hire a professional coach in certain challenging periods of their lives, and then take a pause or change to a different coach. There's nothing wrong with that kind of an approach.

Just make sure you don't try to run away to a different coach right at the moment when a coach gives you a tougher exercise to do. Then you may have a problem with execution, not with the coach.

–MENTORING PROGRAMS

You can also find many different mentoring programs online, and probably in your local community as well. Mentoring programs can be only matching programs or even more: some do matching as well as provide a framework to give the best possible result of mentoring sessions.

Besides matching, frameworks and individual sessions, you can also find many group mentoring and mastermind group formation services, and all other kind of different specialized mentoring programs. Many of them provide really good services. Again, there's no other option but to try it and see for yourself. If such programs work for you, great, if not, find a new option. There are many of them available. Just don't waste time on what doesn't work and instead persevere at things that work for you best.

CHAPTER 9:

ORGANIZING A PLAN

Have you ever been in a situation where you needed to complete several tasks in a very short amount of time? What was the first thing you did? Most of us may have jumped right in tackling the projects while gathering tools and supplies along the way. Although this seems to be the productive course of action, there is a more efficient way that will save you time, energy, and effort. Start first by organizing a plan. When done correctly, your plan will be a Progressive Layout of All Necessities (P-L-A-N). Then prioritize the plan so that it will automatically align itself with the goal.

Some days, we may find ourselves in a neutral state where we feel focused and motivated, but yet we just can't seem to move forward with our plans. Why does this happen? Often, this means that there is something missing or simply out of place. When we rethink the plan, more times than not, we will find that our plans, in fact, are just out of order. If we start implementing a plan that is out of order, it can sometimes lead us off-course or slightly deter us from the goal.

Remember the P in PLAN. Progressive is the momentum that keeps all necessities moving forward. Each step of a good plan will support its following action. Re-evaluate the plan to see if each step or action gets you closer to the goal. Think of a tall building: if the first floor isn't properly planned, it becomes virtually impossible to add the second floor. Always visualize your goal just as a portraitist often looks at a subject. The more detail you can see about the goal, the easier it becomes to build a successful plan.

Just as in business, a mission statement is useless without a plan to execute on it. You too should develop and write down your personal and professional plan, including short term and long term goals. This plan will not and should not be penned and framed, as it is organic and will change as your personal and professional circumstances change. The purpose here is to have a clear understanding of what you want to accomplish personally and how you will achieve it.

Many individuals claim they focus on planning and effectiveness, but there is a considerable difference between merely claiming or intending to do so, and actually enhancing their performance and using their plans effectively, so as to implement the best possible plan in order to fully maximize their potential. Our greatest plans become infinitely more attainable, when we focus on the 4 C's.

1. **_Consider:_** Don't proceed without planning effectively, and to do so, you must truly consider what you hope to address or improve, and how your plan might move you towards your goals! Think about the needs, concerns, priorities and best interests of the organization and constituents you serve!

2. **_Choose:_** Begin the thought process, by opting for the course of action which might provide the greatest possibilities! Know your options, including the pros and cons, and focus on getting prepared and ready.

3. **_Create:_** Planning becomes irrelevant without taking action, in a timely and well-prepared manner! A true leader must take the responsibility, and move his group forward towards its goal, in line with a vibrant, vital vision. This can only occur when one develops a well-considered plan, and creates and implements it, in a carefully crafted, motivating, engaging way, that also provides the best foreseeable possibility for success.

4. **_Seek consensus:_** Appeal to the best in all stakeholders. Seek common ground, which focuses on achieving whatever is in the best interest of the organization. Rather than merely diluting, compromising, and attempting to be popular, communicate and articulate, in an empathetic manner, why you have opted for a particular course of action, and its benefits.

CHAPTER 10:

SEEKING SUPPORT

Let's utilize the support of others. We are the to-doers who are often tasked with getting the job done! This is actually a great thing, as it shows us that others have the confidence in our abilities to succeed. We must however not focus on the frustrations of the goal but rather on the objective itself. Instead of compiling tasks for ourselves, let's utilize the help of others and build a team where a balanced workload can be dispersed among our talented supporters. To do this requires us to be organized leaders that not only lead by example but also become the driven initiative that motivates the cause.

Chapter 11:

Become An Effective Leader

Being organized, and harnessing the ability to lead by example, is the key to motivating and driving others to be successful. There are many people in high positions who bark orders and expect them to get done. These same people probably haven't been in the trenches, so to speak, for a long time. They are far removed from daily tasks. While this is not necessarily wrong, it may not be the best way to motivate people.

Contrast that style with someone who digs in. For example, if you have a manager that contributes to the group but does so without getting in the way, this is one who is leading by example. Teams usually respond much easier to this style of leadership. It's a no-nonsense approach, and it shows the team that you care about getting things done.

Of course, if managers get too involved to the point where they are actually micromanaging everyone's tasks, this can be just as bad as the manager that takes no involvement in the process. It's okay for a manager to step in once in a while when a team member is struggling, or when there is a shortage of staff on the team. But when it gets to the point when the manager is meddling, it will cause problems for the team and the morale will take a hit.

However, when the manager does get the balance right, there can be great harmony among the team members. Apart from that, it also removes any excuses that some of the members may try to use. It's going to be difficult to get away with not doing something when a manager is ready and able to do it himself. This can be good for the team, though, as they will be motivated to get more work completed and on time. It all depends on the talent of the team as well as the type of project that is being worked on. If the team consists of veterans of the field, they won't need much manager intervention, and in fact, the manager will probably slow them down in this instance. If the industry they are working with is complicated, like engineering, the manager may not even have the skills needed to be of help. In this case, the manager should offer ancillary support, like making sure the team has what it needs, and buffering them from having to deal with outside forces. A team should be able to figure out its own dynamic over time and managers should let that happen as much as possible. Good managers will know how to gauge this and give the right kind of help at the appropriate time.

To demonstrate respect and equip others, we need to practice the following skills with people:

1. Become a Fully Connected Listener

Listening shows respect and appreciation. Listening must come first and it requires patience. "The opposite of talking is waiting." Our natural desire to talk, judge others, our biased ego, and our business, all inhibit our inclination to listen. "The less we worry about appearing smart, the smarter we will appear to be by just listening and asking smart questions."

Listening is easier when we are curious. It's easier too when you know and believe in your purpose for listening. More than just gathering information, "when you listen to someone, you learn how that person thinks, which provides insight into how you can use them most effectively on a project, team, or in the organization."

Listen for intent and observe body language. Much of what you need to know is communicated in this way. Respect others by taking a breath and listen to what they have to say. "When we're great listeners, we give others the gift of silence. We're not in a hurry, so silence and time to think gives the speaker the opportunity to formulate and express his or her best thinking."

2. Ask Powerful Questions

When you ask questions, you become more engaging and it creates bonds with others. It means they will want to listen to you.

The right questions are important. "The right question is often a crystallizer. It helps put a bow of clarity around one's thoughts." It can help them to articulate their own thoughts and expand their thinking. Clarity questions are "What concerns you most about this?" "If there is one thing you could do to begin to resolve this issue, what is it?" "What are your instincts telling you?" Timing matters when you are asking questions and you should ask when you need clarity.

Great questions open the door to additional thoughts. For instance, a question like "Is this the solution?" opens the door to additional thoughts but closes the door on the conversation. A better question would be "If there is one thing that would make this solution better, what will it be?" The response, "I have not thought about that" is one of the best you can receive from your questions. You're giving the other person the opportunity to think about new solutions in a positive way. You are also showing respect for the person being asked the question.

3. Develop the Best Thinking of Others

Great listening and questions lead others from "I don't get it" to "I got it." It allows you to bring out the best in others. By helping others grow, you give them the opportunity to take ownership of their actions and the results. That's a prime example of leading.

Be forward-thinking and solution oriented. "When leaders focus on what can be done, people are inspired to achieve more, especially when they think of and articulate what it is that they are going to do."

One of the best ways to inspire your team to follow you because of you rather than in spite of you is to acknowledge the things they do well. More than a compliment, by acknowledging someone, you are "calling attention to a specific behavior or talent, and it comes without any type of extra modifiers."

4. Wise and Thoughtful Delegation

Delegating demonstrates that you believe in others and they often respond by "expanding their ability to do more and perform at a higher level."

As a leader, the more you put everyone in the sweet spots of their talents, including you, the greater the likelihood of achieving short- and long-term exceptional performance. Delegating wisely both develops and efficiently utilizes those talents.

Thinking we can do it better, impatience, a lack of trust, and a lack of clarity about the job to be done all inhibit our desire to delegate tasks. And that's on us.

CHAPTER 12:

DISORGANIZATION AND STRESS

Let's think about stress and how it affects us every day. Stress sometimes makes us just want to get away from the things that we ultimately must deal with. Have you ever thought about why we want to go on vacation or take extended breaks from our day-to-day lives? Usually in some way, shape or form, this means that we need to de-stress. This can also indicate that our passions are being shadowed by doubt.

Stress, in most cases, is not a good thing to have in our lives; however, it is how we deal with it that makes us succeed or fail. Now, you may be thinking that stress is never a good thing, right? What if we convert that stress into an immediate positive notion? We can do this by looking at stress from a different angle. What if we see our stress as a challenge? Challenges are often embraced whereas stresses are ignored. If we can create a challenge out of stress, we can actually remove doubt and boost confidence.

Stress is something I've faced in a deep and personal way, and have overcome successfully. Living with stress is surprisingly common, according to the

American Psychological Association, approximately 60% of Americans are stressed with concerns over money, job pressure and health contributing to 76% of stress.

Numerous studies have shown that stress has a strong negative impact on well-being and prolonged stress has been associated with anxiety, depression, coronary diseases and sleep problems.

It's clear that to live a happy and fulfilled life, we need to learn how to respond to life's challenges without getting overly stressed. However, stress itself is complicated. Let's examine the real cause of stress and how to manage stress and turn it into success.

Stress is an evolutionary response to a threat in our environment. In our caveman days, stress helped us survive by triggering our 'fight' or 'flight' response to help us run away from wild animals or fight to defend our territory.

In today's modern world however, stress has evolved as a coping mechanism to help us manage mental and emotional overwhelm such as dealing with demanding bosses, managing our finances or surviving health issues. As these are daily problems, we simply do not have the emotional strength and mind space to respond effectively each and every day; this is how stress becomes chronic and starts to interfere with our lives.

Symptoms of feeling stressed

Symptoms of stress can be very obvious or buried deep in our psyche depending on how we've dealt with stressful experiences through our lives.

Overt (or obvious) symptoms of stress

Symptoms of stress commonly manifest in terms of physical, mental or emotional discomfort.

• Physical signs include headaches, tiredness, an upset stomach or an inability to sleep well

• Mental signs include feeling overwhelmed, being 'down in the dumps' and unable to enjoy yourself or switch off

• Emotional signs include being irritable, impatient, anxious, nervous, depressed, lonely and feeling like there's no way out

CONCLUSION

Have a Dream: You need to have dreams. Without it there would be nothing much to fire up your motivation to achieve. Only if you have a dream will you work to make it a reality.

Maintain a Positive attitude: Positive thinking helps build a positive attitude, which will increase your energy levels and make you work harder to achieve your goals. You should keep away from negative thoughts or people propagating them.

Maintain Consistency: You should work with commitment and stability. With difficulties cropping up in between, you may get discouraged after initial excitement when you started. You therefore need to guard against discouragement creeping in and always remain focused.

Start with a small step: A lot of planning goes into initiating steps toward your goal. People with dreams have all their plans ready for achieving them but they find it very challenging to take initial steps. You must build up courage and begin your journey towards your goal and once you begin it is not that difficult to continue.

Avoid Procrastination: You should avoid laziness and work towards achieving your daily targets in order to achieve your goal. Small breaks in between will keep you fresh and energetic. Also, you should always avoid delaying or postponing things to the next day.

Never call it Quits: If planning is right and goals are achievable, you may surely gain success and achieve your goal. There may be times when things will not move in the way you want. In such situations you should never lose hope and must carry on with your aim.

Writing this book has allowed me to express myself with words that enlighten the pathways between my thoughts and visions. There are many important people that have contributed to my desire to achieve, focus to thrive, and ambition to go for it!

My Mother and Father have always seen in me what I could not see. They have given me the tools and structure to achieve greatness yet I always wondered what that was… Over the years I've learned that the foundation of my legacy is having their love and Motivational Drive to be Successful.

Thank You Mom & Dad for being mine!

I'd also like to thank those that have inspired my creativity & determination… Chauncey Tanksley, Chelcey Williams, Tracey Williams, Cherie Tullis, Tim Carigan, Hershey James, Rick & Lisa Briggs, Doc Evans, Crazy Terry, Mark Lanz, Pete Rodriguez, Shawn Randolph, Darren Reames, Mike Javius, Julius Brown, Daren Wright, Larry Morten, Michael & Ericka Smith.

Often we go through life not knowing why we meet or cross paths with certain people. Its like seeing an exotic car in the mall and wondering why it's there… You just can't help yourself but you must get closer to check it out. That's exactly how I felt when I met my friend Taylor Lamasky. She has the personality of a just popped locker room champagne bottle!

Taylor your enthusiasm and positive energy gives me the boost to keep writing!

ABOUT THE AUTHOR

Andre D. Jackson was born and raised in the San Francisco Bay Area and is a Vocal Coach at SoundCap Audio. Some would say that he's a Jack of all trades… He has worked as a motivational speaker, director of sales, an entrepreneur, movie actor and voice over specialist, amongst others.

Andre is a new author and this book, **Motivation Drives Success**, is a self-help title that is aimed at inspiring others to find the success in life that has been eluding them. This is just the first volume of a planned series and Andre has several others in the pipeline that he has high hopes for.

In his free time, Andre enjoys reading, singing, camping and cooking. He loves to get out into the fresh air whenever he gets the opportunity, occasionally taking to the water and boating, while in the past he has also devoted some of his spare hours as a volunteer fireman, giving something back to his local community.

In the future, he hopes to continue with the good work he has been doing, motivating and inspiring others to do great things through his writing and speaking engagements.

Do not go yet; One last thing to do

If you enjoyed this book or found it useful I'd be very grateful if you'd post a short review on it. Your support really does make a difference and I read all the reviews personally so I can get your feedback and make this book even better.

Thanks again for your support!